The Wild Side of Pet
Birds

Jo Waters

www.raintreepublishers.co.uk
Visit our website to find out more information about **Raintree** books.

To order:
☎ Phone 44 (0) 1865 888112
▤ Send a fax to 44 (0) 1865 314091
▢ Visit the Raintree Bookshop at **www.raintreepublishers.co.uk** to browse our catalogue and order online.

First published in Great Britain by Raintree,
Halley Court, Jordan Hill, Oxford OX2 8EJ,
part of Harcourt Education.
Raintree is a registered trademark of Harcourt
Education Ltd.

Editorial: Melanie Copland and Sarah Chappelow
Design: Richard Parkerand Tinstar Design Ltd
    (www.tinstar.co.uk)
Illustrations: Jeff Edwards
Picture Research: Mica Brancic and
    Charlotte Lippmann
Production: Duncan Gilbert

Originated by Ambassador Litho Ltd
Printed and bound in China by South China
Printing Company

ISBN 1 8444 3929 1
08 07 06 05
10 9 8 7 6 5 4 3 2 1

**British Library Cataloguing in
Publication Data**
Waters, Jo
The Wild Side of Pet Birds
636.6'8
A full catalogue record for this book is available
from the British Library.

Acknowledgements
The publishers would like to thank the following
for permission to reproduce photographs: Ardea
p. **7** (John Daniels); Bruce Coleman p. **27**; Corbis
pp. **5**, **15**; Digital Stock p. **14**; Digital Vision p.
8, **22**; FLPA pp. **4**, **11**; Getty Images/Photodisc
p. **6**; Harcourt Education Ltd/Tudor Photography
p. **25**, **29**; Nature Picture Library p. **5** (Ulrike
Schanz), **23** (Ulrike Schanz), **24** (Tony Heald);
NHPA pp. **9** (Joe Blossom), **10** (Alan Williams),
16 (Bill Coster), **19** (Manfred Danegger), **20**
(Stephen Dalton), **21** (Stephen Dalton), **26**
(Hellio & Van Ingen), **28** (Daniel Heuclin);
RSPCA Photolibrary p. **17** (Joe Blossom).
Cover photograph of a pet yellow crowned
Amazon parrot reproduced with permission of
Nature Picture Library (Ulrike Schanz). Inset
cover photograph of a bald eagle in flight
reproduced with permission of NHPA (Stephen
Dalton).

The publishers would like to thank Michaela
Miller for her assistance in the preparation of this
book.

Every effort has been made to contact copyright
holders of any material reproduced in this book.
Any omissions will be rectified in subsequent
printings if notice is given to the publishers.

Contents

Any words appearing in bold, **like this**, are explained in the Glossary.

Was your pet once wild?

You may think that you just have a pet bird, but the birds people keep as pets are very close to their wild relatives. Finding out more about the wild side of your pet bird will help you give it a better life.

There are many different types of wild bird. You may see wild birds every day in your garden, in cities, and in the country.

Wild parakeets roost in **flocks**.

People have kept birds as pets for over 4000 years. There are many types of bird that are kept as pets. Budgerigars are good companions because they are naturally very **sociable** birds.

Birds can be kept in **aviaries** or large cages. They need everyday care, including feeding, exercise, and cleaning.

Pet birds, like this Hahn's macaw, are very similar to their wild relatives.

Types of bird

There are as many as 10,000 different **species** of wild bird.

Flightless birds
Some birds cannot fly. These include emus, ostriches, kiwis, penguins, rheas, and cassowaries.

Scientists group birds by the **habitat** they live in. More than half of all birds **perch** on branches and are known as perching birds. Birds that live mostly on the ground are called running birds. Birds, like penguins, that live in or near water are called **aquatic** birds.

Flamingos are wading birds.

6

Different sizes

Birds can be as big as an ostrich, which weighs up to 155 kilograms (342 pounds), or as small as a wren, which only weighs about 10 grams (less than 1 ounce).

The right pet?
*Think carefully before choosing a bird as a pet. Birds like parrots live for a long time and need lots of space as they are very active. Some **exotic** birds are not suitable pets as they are difficult to care for properly.*

Pet birds are all related to wild ones. Some are better **adapted** for living as pets than others. Imagine keeping a pet ostrich!

Budgerigars, canaries, parakeets, and zebra finches like these can all be kept as pets.

7

Where are birds from?

Birds live all over the world – in forests, deserts, the frozen Arctic and Antarctic, and even the seas and oceans. The wandering albatross can spend months in the air without ever landing!

Common European and American birds to look out for include robins, pigeons, finches, tits, thrushes, blackbirds, and magpies. In Australia, galahs, budgerigars, and parakeets are common in the wild.

The toucan is a **rainforest** bird.

Choosing your pet

When you have decided that a bird is the right pet for you, you will need to find out more. Your local vet will be able to give you some advice.

These lovebirds are in good condition.

Never buy birds that have been caught from the wild, as this is cruel. Always try to get your pets from a good **breeder**.

When you are choosing your pet bird, make sure it is in good condition. Check that it has healthy feathers, clean limbs, and a strong beak. Its claws should not be overgrown, it should have clear, bright eyes, and be active and alert.

Bird habitats

Birds have **adapted** to live in all parts of the world. Different **species** live in all **climates** and **habitats**.

Northern Europe and America have cool climates and habitats, such as snowy mountains and open grasslands. Birds like the golden eagle and pheasant live there.

Tropical birds, like macaws and toucans, live in habitats such as rainforests and jungles.

Many birds live near or over seas, oceans, rivers, and lakes. Some examples are ducks and kingfishers.

The kingfisher's beak is specially adapted to catching fish.

An aviary has lots of room for pet birds to fly about.

Bird homes

You must try to give pet birds all the things they would need in the wild. Just like wild birds, pet birds need to exercise. The best place to keep them is in an **aviary.**

All aviaries and cages need to be cleaned regularly. You must clean out any droppings and old food or dirty water.

Baths!

Pet birds, just like their wild relatives, need to keep clean. Some wash themselves in a bowl of water. Others like to be gently sprayed with water from a water bottle.

11

Bird anatomy

All birds have wings and feathers. Each **species** looks different because its **anatomy** has **adapted** to where it lives and what it eats.

Birds that fly long distances, like swifts and gulls, are **streamlined** to help them glide through the air. Birds that swim, like geese, are fatter and heavier because they spend more time just floating on the water.

Feather design
Birds have smooth, strong flight feathers on their wings, fluffy down feathers for keeping warm and colourful tail and head feathers for displaying.

This drawing shows the skeleton of a bird.

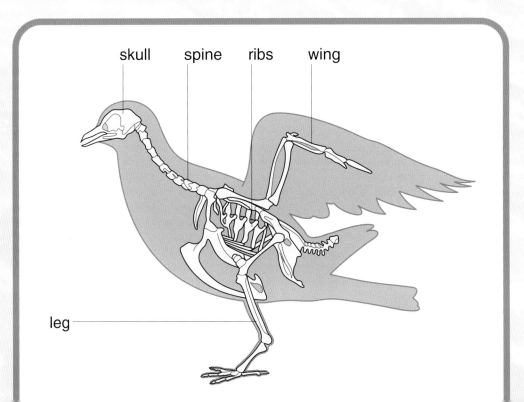

skull   spine   ribs   wing

leg

12

Colours

Pet birds have the same anatomy as wild birds. But **breeders** have bred them specially to make them look different. Wild budgerigars are green or yellow, but pet ones come in many different greens, yellows, whites, blues, and greys.

Birds like budgerigars have special beaks that never stop growing. If they are not worn down, they get overgrown and can stop the bird eating. These birds need to **gnaw** at things to keep their beaks in shape. Cuttlefish, millet, and rough wood are all good for gnawing.

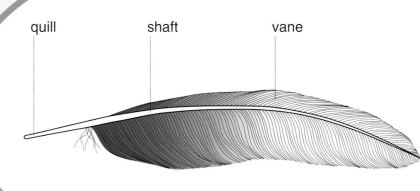

quill   shaft   vane

Feathers come in many shapes, sizes, and colours, but they all have the same basic design.

Senses

Birds have very sensitive senses, but rely mostly on sight and hearing. They use these to avoid **predators** in the wild and to find food.

Predator birds, like owls and eagles, have eyes at the front of their heads because this is best for spotting their **prey**. Most other birds have eyes at the sides of their heads. This is so they can see all around them to keep alert for danger.

This barn owl's eyes are specially **adapted** for hunting in the dark.

All birds have ears at the sides of their heads, although you can't see them. Hearing is very important for communicating and sensing danger. Owls use hearing to pinpoint their prey.

Pet birds use their ears to listen to other birds and people.

All birds can see well in colour. Wild hummingbirds use this to find the right flowers to feed from. Parrots use it to find the right food to eat.

Pet hummingbirds should be given **nectar** bottles with a red spouts, as this colour appeals to them.

Movement

Birds like parrots and finches use their wings to fly and claws and beaks to climb. Water birds, such as ducks and swans float on the water and use webbed feet to push themselves along.

Birds also use their claws to grab **prey** and their beaks to break shells or carry things like nesting materials.

Flying under water!

Penguins and cormorants are at home under water as well as above it. They both use their wings to swim under the water when they dive for fish.

Gannets dive into the water and grab fish in their beaks.

Pet birds use their wings to fly, just as they would in the wild.

Parrots, parakeets, and cockatoos will also use their beaks and claws to climb around their **aviaries**.

Perching

*Most pet birds are **perching** birds. This means they need a perch to rest on. A perch should be wide and made of wood. Plastic ones can have sharp bits which hurt the birds' feet.*

Cockatoos like to climb, and will even climb on you if you let them! Be careful as their beaks and claws are sharp.

What do birds eat?

Wild birds eat all sorts of things. Birds of **prey**, like owls, hunt for small animals. Kookaburras kill and eat snakes and worms. Blackbirds and thrushes eat worms and insects. Finches and tits eat seeds, fruit, and nuts.

Nectar and pollen
*Birds like lories, lorikeets, and hummingbirds, eat the **pollen** and **nectar** made by flowers.*

Many **tropical** birds eat fruit and nuts. Macaws have specially designed beaks for breaking open nuts and tearing fruit.

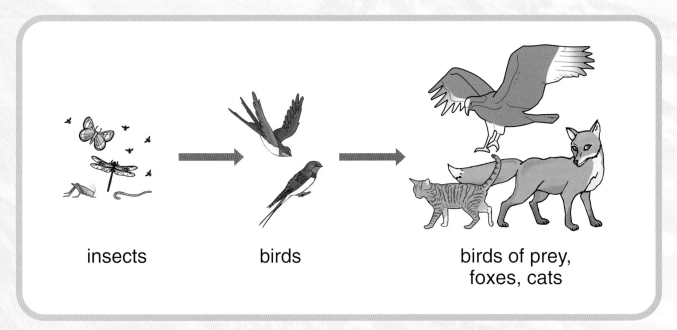

insects   birds   birds of prey,
foxes, cats

Birds fit into a **food chain** like this.

Pet birds need to eat what they would in the wild. Make sure you find out exactly what kind of food your pet birds need to eat. You can get most bird foods, including fruit, seeds, and live foods, at a good pet shop.

Your pet should always have a clean supply of fresh water. A water dropper bottle is best for this as the water stays fresh and clean.

Pet cockatiels need to have seed to eat in their aviary.

Food colouring!

*Some **breeds** of canary are naturally a pale yellow colour. Some foods, like carrots, can make that colour even stronger!*

Hunting and exercise

Wild birds stay alert most of the time. They are very active, flying, hunting or searching for food.

Migration

*Some birds **migrate** to other countries in different seasons. This can be to find food or to **breed**.*

Birds of **prey**, like kestrels, hover to spot and hunt their prey. Then they dive and catch it on the ground.

Hummingbirds hover over flowers and drink the **nectar**. Their wings move so fast you can only see a blur.

Some birds, like this swallow, catch insects to eat while they fly through the air.

Exercising

Pet birds cannot hunt or migrate, but they still need exercise. Birds kept in cages can get bored very easily if they cannot explore or do different things. This can make them stressed and ill. They may chew their cages or even pluck out their feathers.

Make sure you can catch your pet before you let it out!

You should always make sure your pet's home is as big as possible. Many people let their birds out of their cages to fly in the home.

Do birds live in groups?

Many wild birds live in groups and are very **sociable**. Groups of birds are called flocks. Birds that live in flocks include parakeets, budgerigars, finches, and galahs.

Birds that live alone or in pairs include **predators**, such as owls. Birds like swans and albatrosses usually live in pairs and **mate** for life.

Flocking

*Many birds flock together when flying. Watch geese flying, especially when they are **migrating**. They fly in a V shape. One goose leads until it is tired, and then another takes over, and so on.*

Penguins nest in large groups called colonies.

Socializing

Just like wild birds, most pet birds need company. Young birds are tamed very easily and see their owner as a member of the flock. **Grooming** and handling your pet bird helps it to make friends with you.

Lovebirds, budgies, cockatiels, and doves are all very sociable. They should all live in groups. A lonely bird can go off its food and be very unhappy. Be very careful if you do introduce a new bird to a group because it may get attacked or bullied.

Try to keep birds of the same size together so that small ones do not get bullied.

Sleeping

Some birds **roost**. They find a safe spot in a tree or cliff and **perch** for the night. Rooks roost in trees, and the place is called a 'rookery'. Eagles' nests and roosts are called 'eyries'.

Seabirds rest on cliffs, rocks, and islands. Many seabirds will rest on the waves when it is calm. Some, like the wandering albatross, can even doze while they are gliding in the air!

Birds like owls are **nocturnal**. They hunt at night and sleep in the day.

Wild birds all need to sleep.

Pet birds need rest and sleep at night too. They also need to be able to rest or nap during the day.

Most pet birds are **tropical** birds. In the wild, they only get 12 hours of daylight a day. Cover their cage in the evening to make it dark, even if you have the lights on.

Pet birds roost on their perches.

In the wild, birds wake at dawn. Like their wild relatives, pet birds are most alert in the early morning. This is the best time to feed them. They will probably also sing most in the morning.

Life cycle of birds

Many **species** of bird live longer as pets then they would in the wild. Canaries can live for up to 15 years in **captivity** and parrots can live to be over 50!

Mating for life
Some birds like bald eagles find a partner and stay with them for the rest of their lives.

Birds have young by laying eggs. The eggs are **incubated** in a nest until the chicks hatch out. The parents feed and look after them until they are fledged (feathered) and old enough to leave the nest.

Osprey parents bring food back to the nest for their young.

Breeding

It is best not to **breed** pet birds. The best way to stop them breeding is to keep females and males apart.

*It is very difficult to tell what sex your pet bird is. Sometimes their **plumage** can be different. In other species, males behave differently to females. Ask your **breeder** or vet to tell you.*

If your pet bird becomes pregnant, it will need somewhere to nest and incubate its eggs. It should be kept very warm, clean, and quiet. Budgerigars usually lay about 6–8 eggs, which take 18 days to hatch.

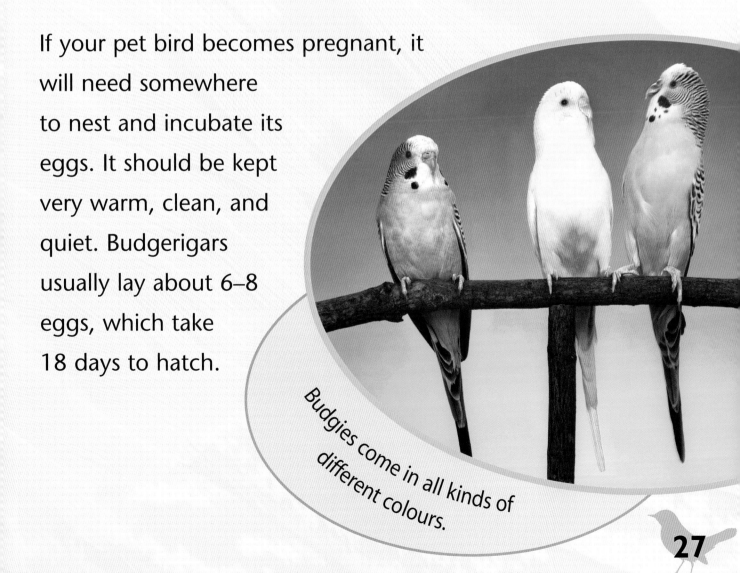

Budgies come in all kinds of different colours.

Common problems

In the wild, birds are often eaten by **predators**, and are also hunted and eaten by people. They can be hurt if their **habitat** is destroyed, for example the **rainforests** are being cut down to make farming land. This is leaving thousands of birds without homes.

In danger!
These birds are **endangered**:
- *Spix's macaw*
- *African fish eagle*
- *Bird of paradise*
- *Hyacinth macaw*
- *California condor*

Birds can also suffer from disease in the wild.

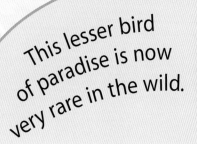

This lesser bird of paradise is now very rare in the wild.

These are some common bird problems.

scaly face

moulting

parasites

Itches and sneezes

Birds can get **parasites**. These include worms inside them and fleas or ticks on their skin.

Budgies can get something called scaly face. This is also caused by a parasite. Your vet can give you something to treat parasites.

Moulting is when the bird loses its feathers. Some loss is natural, but if your bird starts losing lots of feathers or plucks them out, it might be ill or bored.

Now you know more about why birds behave the way they do, you can look forward to a rewarding future with your birds.

Find out for yourself

A good owner will always want to learn more about keeping pet birds. To find out more information about birds, you can look in other books and on the Internet.

Books to read

Budgerigars (A Complete Pet Owner's Manual), Immanuel Birmelin, Barron's Educational Series, 1998

Caring for Your Pet Budgies (Pet Care series), Don Harper, Interpet Publishing, 1999

Using the Internet

Explore the Internet to find out about birds. Websites can change, so if one of the links below no longer works, don't worry. Use a search engine, such as *www.yahooligans.com* or *www.internet4kids.com*. You could try searching using the key words 'bird', 'pet', and 'wild birds'.

Websites

A good site for finding out more about wild birds can be found at: *http://www.rspb.org.uk/*

The following site has lots of information about looking after all kinds of pet birds: *http://www.rspca.org.uk*

Disclaimer
All the Internet addresses (URLs) given in this book were valid at the time of going to press. However, due to the dynamic nature of the Internet, some addresses may have changed, or sites may have ceased to exist since publication. While the author and publishers regret any inconvenience this may cause readers, no responsibility for any such changes can be accepted by either the author or the publishers.

Glossary

adapt become used to living in certain conditions

anatomy how the body is made

aquatic to do with water

aviary/aviaries large outdoor cages where birds can live and fly

breed when animals mate and have babies

breeder someone who raises animals

captivity kept in a cage rather than living in the wild

climate the type of weather in a certain place

endangered in danger of dying out or being killed

exotic colourful and unusual

food chain links between animals that feed on each other

gnaw to chew, bite, or nibble

groom to clean an animal

habitat where an animal or plant lives

incubate to keep eggs warm until they hatch

mate when two animals come together to make babies

migrate to fly to another country for summer or winter

nectar sugary liquid produced by flowers

nocturnal awake at night

parasites tiny animals that live in or on another animal

perch when birds stand on a branch and grip with their feet

plumage feathers

pollen special dust in flowers

predator animal that hunts and eats other animals

prey animals that are hunted and eaten by predators

rainforest thick tropical forest

roost when birds sleep on a perch at night

scientists people who study the world and nature

sociable likes company

species types of similar animals that can have babies together

streamlined slim and smooth so it moves through the air easily

tropical warm parts of the earth near the equator

Index

Titles in the *Wild Side of Pets* series include:

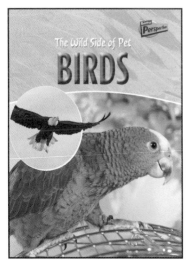

Hardback   1844439291

Hardback   184443933X

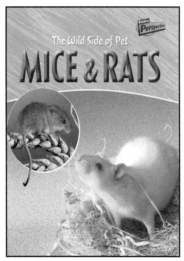

Hardback   1844439305

Hardback   1844439313

Hardback   1844439321

Find out about the other titles in this series on our website www.raintreepublishers.co.uk